Remember ABERGAVENNY

including the villages of Crickhowell, Gilwern, Govilon, Llanellen, Llanfoist and Llanover

Volume 1

by Louis Bannon

This book is dedicated to my dear parents
Louis and Julia Bannon.

Old Bakehouse Publications

Abertillery

First published in November 1995

ISBN 1 874538 751

Published in the U.K. by
Old Bakehouse Publications
Church Street,
Abertillery, Gwent NP3 1EA
Telephone: 01495 212600   Fax: 01495 216222

Made and printed in the UK
by J.R. Davies (Printers) Ltd.

Foreword

by Alan Breeze
Mayor of Abergavenny 1980-81 and 1985-86

It is a great pleasure to write a foreword to this book.

We owe a debt of gratitude to Louis Bannon for producing this splendid pictorial record which is the result of a great deal of time and effort on his part over many years.

Thanks to Louis' dedication, we are able to follow in vivid visual detail the recent history of our town. The various pictures will undoubtedly evoke many memories, some happy and some sad, of Abergavenny and its people.

I am sure that we will all share in the feelings of nostalgia, love and pride that Louis Bannon has for his home town. His reward will be our enjoyment of this book.

Foreword

by Peter Williams
Founder Chairman - Monuments Restoration Fund
St Mary's Priory Church, Abergavenny

It is said that there is a book in all of us. Have we not been tempted to put pen to paper? In our book-shop browsing, have we at some stage muttered, 'I could do that!'

We never do start our book, because we soon realise that it will be just too much hard work and we are not prepared to face the hundreds of hours researching, collecting information, checking for accuracy and finally presenting a document which will be attractive and interesting.

Louis Bannon had been gathering his collection of postcards of Abergavenny and surrounding area for many years. He has taken great pride in his very wide private collection - a vivid pictorial record of his town.

Now Louis has chosen to share with us his hobby of many years, and not for commercial gain, because he has pledged further financial support to the Monuments Restoration Programme in St Mary's Priory Church, through the sales of his book.

The Restoration Fund started on the 28th November 1991 and Louis and his fellow market traders, made the very first donation of £400 that night. Louis was aware, as of course others were, of the urgency for a restoration scheme to save the town's treasures and had persuaded his colleagues to help.

So well done Louis, you have completed 'your' book and I recommend 'Remember Abergavenny' as a book of wide interest. It will certainly rouse the memories of older residents and will be of great interest to everyone who has come to live in or to visit the Gateway to Wales.

Introduction

Having for the past twenty years roamed the country searching for postcards of my home town of Abergavenny and surrounding areas, I have finally succumbed to the requests of my friends to publish a book and here it is!

For the non postcard collector I am sure that the prospect of travelling miles in search of 'just one more' must appear to be extremely boring - a philosophy, my wife would agree with, and yet a rare topic on which we beg to differ. Nothing gets the adrenalin pumping quite as much as the exploration through endless boxes of postcards marked 'Wales' or 'Gwent' as one seeks for that elusive card. Neither does it end there of course. Having located a new specimen, one then has to spend hour upon hour researching its history and thus, the appetite becomes yet further whetted.

This thirst for knowledge of one's home town has led me to travel the length and breadth of this country and even abroad, in pursuit of even more cards and photographs to add to the ever increasing numbers in my collection. The hobby becomes an obsession. This obsession of mine, I would now like to share with you in the pages of this book.

Never having attempted anything quite like this before, I have surveyed my collection and randomly chosen those cards which I consider tell the story of the development of this historic town of ours. I hope that many of those selected will be new to the reader and perhaps result in a great deal of nostalgia, as we wander down memory lane.

I very often picture myself standing on a street corner at the turn of this century, watching life as it was then. The horse and cart as modes of transport dominate the scene; gas lamps are conspicuous and the gas lighter is also to be seen going about his business.

Moving on ten years, we begin to see how things are starting to change. The commencement of the Great War approaches; the usurpation of the horse and cart by the motor car; the changes in fashion are all recorded in these cards.

For many years, before and after the First World War, this area was used as a military training ground. Regiments came from all over Britain arriving at one of the three railway stations to be found in the town at that time. This must have been an incredible boost to business in the area.

Through the pages we are able to advance a few decades and now find ourselves at the approach of World War Two. Looking at the same scene now, we see that the motor car has well and truly established itself, electricity has arrived and yet again, fashions have changed! You begin to realise that nothing ever does remain the same and suddenly it becomes important to document the changes so that future generations of Abergavenny will be able to appreciate the history that they have inherited. It is my hope that through the publication of this book, I am assisting the work of those who have tried to do the same.

Over the last four decades the town has changed enormously. The railways are no longer the large employer that they once were. Two of the three railway stations have now disappeared; people's shopping habits change. Having traded in Abergavenny's market for well over 25 years, I have witnessed a decline in its importance. Long gone are the 'miners holidays' when the town would be packed with an influx of colliers from the valleys, intent on purchasing a few bargains at Bannon's stall. No, today we live in a world of consumerism and fast food, with no time for browsing. We live in an age where the multi national flourish and the small business person struggles hard to stay afloat, many having given up the ghost and moved on to pastures new. The spectre of 'out of town supermarkets' has arrived to add maybe, to the decay of the town?

Whatever your views are on that very controversial issue, one thing is certain, we live in and belong to a very beautiful part of Wales. Nothing can ever change that!

A donation from the proceeds of this book is being given to the 'Monuments Restoration Fund' in order to help in preserving them for future generations.

Louis Bannon

Contents

CHAPTER 1

Abergavenny Town

1. The aerial view of the town of Abergavenny makes an ideal start to the book and will enable readers to study and reflect on how much change has taken place since this photograph was taken some 60 years ago.

2. An early photograph of Frogmore Street. With the number of people in evidence this could well be market day. Note the cabs waiting at the cab stand in front of the Baptist Chapel.

3. A later photograph of the same view. The cab stand has now disappeared and has been replaced by the War Memorial but the milk is still being delivered by horse and cart! There are a few wreaths to be seen around the monument which suggests that this was taken shortly after Remembrance Sunday.

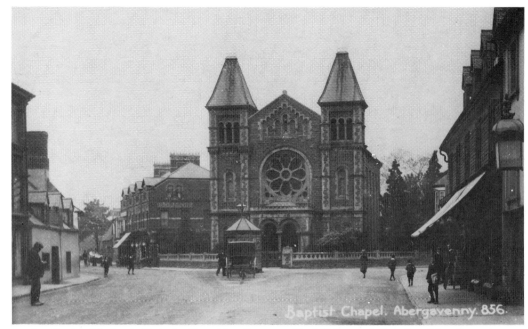

4. On the right hand side is the Chronicle office owned by M Morgan & Co, advertising themselves as booksellers, stationers, bookbinders, fancy repository and newsagents. On the left is the Butchers Arms. Originally an early 17th century half timbered building, it was demolished in the 1960s.

5. The lower end of Frogmore Street and again various types of transport are to be seen. Although this card was posted in 1918, the photograph was taken a lot earlier. On the left hand side is the George Hotel where Richards' store is today.

6. This is a scene of the lower end of Cross Street, photographed in about 1909 with lots of carriages parked on the road. On the right hand side can be seen the old Duke of Wellington Inn which had stables at the rear of the building for housing the horses, the main form of transport at the time. This Abergavenny Inn closed in 1947. On the opposite side of the street can be seen another, now defunct establishment, that of the Capital and Counties bank.

7. The same view 24 years later. The Capital and Counties bank has gone and has been replaced by Moon and Co's garage. Although horses and carts are still evident in the street, the age of the motor car has truly begun. The 'X' on the postcard marks the shop where it would have been purchased.

8. Can you spot anything unusual about this photograph? Although it is on a postcard, which dates from 1900+, the photograph was taken a lot earlier in about 1870, just after the town hall was completed. The tell-tale sign is that the clock face on the town hall has not yet been fitted.

9. A view of Cross Street with Lloyds bank on the right hand side. Next to the bank can be seen the post office with a hand pushed post cart outside and in the centre of the street is the man employed to sweep up the horse manure. C J Daniels operated from the town hall where Concord Discounts have their shop today.

10. The Market Hall and Cross Street as it appeared some 30 years ago. On the right is the former Wheatsheaf public house, whilst next to yet another pub, The White Swan, is the Continental Cafe. The White Swan was owned by Facey & Co Ltd between 1865 and 1879 as a retail outlet for their brewery and wine import business.

11. An interior view of the ever popular Abergavenny market in 1958. To be seen standing in front of the second pillar on the left is Mr Louis Bannon Sr. at his stall selling his foam rubber products. The market hall also hosted boxing and wrestling tournaments for many years. The layout of the market remained virtually unchanged for most of this century until quite recent alterations.

12. A superb view of Market Street with Facey and Sons market brewery visible at the bottom of the street. There is a horse tied up halfway along the street where these days there is a fish and chip shop. At the far end is the building 'Lewis's Dining Rooms' which until recent times was the site of Alan Long's antique shop.

13. Although Frogmore Street and Cross Street are very well photographed, High Street appears to have been left out. This early view is adopted from an original postcard published by Cecil Minson, at one time trading from No. 52 Frogmore Street.

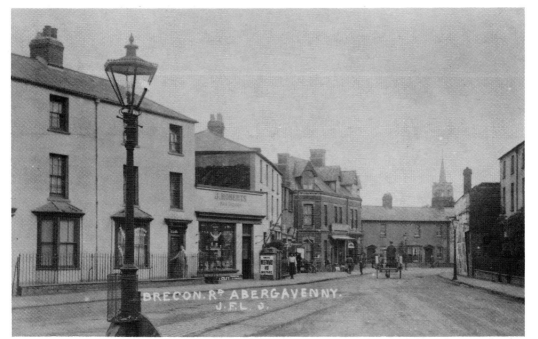

14. A view altered little, except for the rather ornate gas lamp standard perhaps, down Brecon Road. The one exception on the right hand side is the building where 'Trash and Treasure' is now. In 1920, James Roberts ran a hairdressing business where the 'Welsh Dolls House' shop is today, whilst at number 11, James Sayce carried on a bakery business.

15. A photograph looking in the other direction down Brecon Road. A E Tonkins' shop, advertising wholesale and retail groceries, confectioner and tobacconist is where Weatherstones, the TV and video repair shop, is today. The railway bridge over the Brecon Road can just be made out in the centre.

16. The town hall end of High Street, before Red Square and pedestrianisation. The correct name for Red Square is in fact High Cross which local dignitaries would prefer to be used. On the right, a sign for the Greyhound Hotel can be seen. On a tariff souvenir which was produced, it states: 'Accommodation comprises a spacious coffee room, a sitting room, a smoke room, commercial rooms, 18 bedrooms with hot and cold water fittings. The bar is a cosy rendezvous. Special arrangements for wedding parties and other functions are made in a large private dining room. Tariff: Weekly £9.9.0: 19/- per night: 3/3d for bath.'

For today's generation who will not recall pre-decimal currency perhaps, £9.9.0 is £9.45, 19/- is 95p and 3/3d is 16p. More than reasonable prices by today's standards!

17. The other end of High Stret showing numbers 11 to 13 up for sale in 1906. The new owners demolished the buildings seen here and reconstructed the area completely. Today's customer will know that numbers 11 to 13 are now occupied by Stead and Simpson's shoe shop, Featherstone's bakery and Currys Electrical appliances respectively.

18. When this photograph was taken at the turn of the century, folk were able to stand and chat in the middle of the road with little interruption from the town's traffic. Not quite so today, despite partial pedestrianisation of the area. Ruther's shop seen on the left, later moved to premises across the road at numbers 7/8 Frogmore Street where they remained in business until 1937. The Temperance Hotel on the right was managed by J S Jones although the building today houses Rayner's the opticians and Granada Television services.

19. A view down the Brecon Road that has not altered a great deal over this century. The street lighting is somewhat different and hopefully one would not see a pile of horse manure left in the road these days!

20. Another view looking down the Brecon Road with the former railway bridge in view. Marked by the sender of this postcard with an 'x' is the Old North Western Hotel, which was also believed to be known as the Colliers Arms in the 1870s. Also in the vicinity were the Station Hotel and The Railway Hotel all highlighting the need for accommodation in the area due to the close proximity of Brecon Road Station with its travellers and visitors. In 1920 Mr Levi Rogers ran the Railway Hotel and Mr Joseph Wordsworth the Station Hotel.

21. A view up Pen-y-Pound and work has just finished on the Presbyterian Church. The foundation stone was laid in 1906 and work was completed in 1908, shortly before this photograph would have been taken.

22. A view of Hereford Road. This is a postcard which was sent in 1909, not long after the Cottage Hospital was built. Henry Pitt ran a nursery and a landscape gardening business from the old nurseries in Hereford Road. In 1895 he won a medal from the Cardiff Horticultural Society show and in 1897 won first prize in the Ebbw Vale flower show.

23. What was known as the new grounds, in the bottom right hand corner, is Oxford Street, with the post office in view. Emma Bowen was sub Postmistress in 1901 and by 1923 Mrs Mary Isabelle Tutt was the sub mistress.

24. A view from the cemetery in Llanfoist, looking over the railway and town bridges. The large house in the centre of this picture is Linda Vista, the home of James Straker in 1901. Mr Straker was at one time Mayor of Abergavenny and a well known local auctioneer, at first he was in partnership with a Mr Lake and later with William Chadwick. Mr Straker's father John Straker was sworn in as a special constable in The Westgate Hotel in Newport, when the chartists arrived.

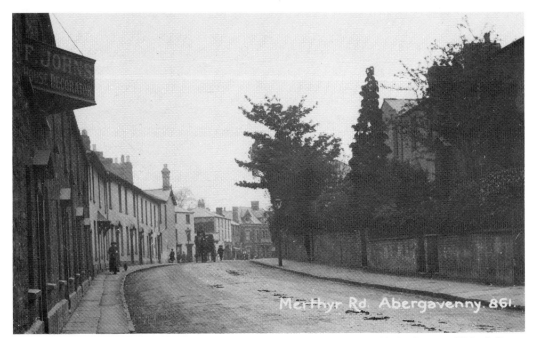

25. Merthyr Road, Abergavenny as it appeared some 90 years before this book was published. On the left can be seen the abode of Mr Frank Johns, the popular house decorator who used the building both as his family home and business office before moving to improved premises at No. 1 Pen-y-Pound. On May 24th 1857, a certain John Fielding was born in Merthyr Road. Later changing his name to John Williams he was awarded the V.C. at the famous battle at Rorke's Drift in the Zulu wars.

26. A snow covered Richmond Road during a winter of many years ago. The house in the centre of this photograph collapsed quite recently during some renovation work.

27. A very early view of Monmouth Road with the Sugar Loaf mountain in the distance. Local readers of this book will note that a number of modern houses have recently been erected near this spot.

28. Early street lighting in Grosvenor Road, which was supplied by the gas works at Merthyr Road. Because Abergavenny Corporation owned the gas works it was not until the 1930s that street lighting changed to electricity. The roads have not yet been laid and one may note the tell-tale signs of horse transport on the primitive roadways.

29. Oakland Road as it appeared to a photographer in about 1907. Today, this area is more familiar as the top end of Park Crescent.

30. Albert Road 1907. On this postcard, sent to Cheltenham, Mr C M Acock tells his wife, 'This is the road we are lodging in. A nice part!'

31. Preston Villa, North Street. In 1901 James Harvey Farquhar occupied this house. He was a solicitor who had an office in Market Street. Among other things, he was also clerk to the rural council and Skenfrith United District School Board.

32. The start of development in Clifton Road, on what was called the New Grounds. Lots of more modern amenities such as street lighting and pavements had yet to arrive when this picture was taken.

33. Frogmore Street runs parallel to Cibbi Brook and suffered badly from flooding and this must have been one of the worst cases. Planks can be seen placed across the road but there do not appear to be too many volunteers. The author has been unable to positively date this catastrophe but there is some evidence on the back of the original photograph that it did happen on a Sunday!

Some readers may remember Boundy the ironmonger's shop seen on the right.

34. Flooding in King Street, December 1929. The houses on the left are where Safeways car park is today. Lion works are in the centre of the photograph which have been replaced by the Argos store. In 1900 Abraham Wyke Harrison ran his mechanical engineering, steam, gas, oil engine manufacturing and dealings in second hand machinery from Lion Street.

35.　Eastman's, of Ebbw Vale took this photograph from Brecon Road Station, showing the back of the houses in Stanhope Street and the allotments where Cantref Road is now.

Cross Street,　Abergavenny.

36.　Always a potentially hazardous junction was that of Monk Street and Cross Street. In May 1913 an important public enquiry was held at the Town Hall with a view to the council raising a loan of £150 to widen Monk Street once and for all. The large shop of Saunders the Seed Merchant seen on the right of this picture fell victim to the demolition plans and the road was eventually widened.

CHAPTER 2

Commercial Interests

37. An early photograph of John Ross and Son in front of their removal van, which they also used as an advertisement on their letter and bill heads as pictured below.

38. This is a 1922 bill head from John Ross & Son. They were listed in the 1920 Kelly's directory as coal and timber merchants as well as haulage contractors. Their address was listed as 4 Victoria Street as well as L & N W R Yard, Brecon Road. The business was taken over by E R Clissold and is today, owned by Messers W G Lane and Sons.

39. This business was established in Abergavenny in 1847, originally as stone masons and later as monumental masons and builders for many years. In 1977 a third branch opened in Brecon and six years later another at Monmouth. In 1990 the take over of businesses in Aberbeeg and Cwmbran gave the company greater coverage in south-east Wales. The Chepstow branch was added in 1992 and Newport, Swansea and Pontypool, followed in 1994. The Company is now the largest independent builders merchant in South Wales.

THE ANGEL
HOTEL, and
POSTING HOUSE,
ABERGAVENNY.

Family and
Commercial.

CARRIAGES & HUNTERS
KEPT FOR HIRE.
TROUT & SALMON
FISHING.

Every convenience
for Motors.

Telephone No. 7.

Proprietor :

H. B. STOCKEN.

40.　An advertisement for the Angel Hotel from the proprietor Hubert Beynon Stocken, who was there from about 1908. In 1920 James Thomas took over. The present owners, Trust House Forte are known to have had an interest in this establishment since 1926.

41.　Something you would not see today. Apart from the lack of cars, nobody would leave their luggage unattended on the pavement outside the Hotel to await collection! The ornate gas standard lamps help make this old view of Cross Street a quite pleasing sight.

42. A group photograph taken in the Angel Hotel's courtyard. Behind the boys is the carriage used to ferry passengers to and from the GWR station. Up until 1950s the present rear car park contained stabling for horses. For most of the 19th century the Angel was a posting inn and office for the mail coaches from London, Milford Haven, Newport, Bristol and Merthyr. Also coaches for Birmingham, Shrewsbury and Aberystwyth stopped here.

Below is an early letter head on a bill from the Angel, when John Pritchard was the proprietor for a period of some 23 years until 1908.

43. This mural was found on the wall of 38 Cross Street, which today houses Greco's Cafe. In the 17th century this building was one wing of the Gunter Mansion. Thomas Gunter, a Catholic, was an attorney who sheltered two priests during the persecution of the Catholics. Father David Lewis and Father Phillip Evans were caught and hung, drawn and quartered at Usk Prison in 1679. This mural may be seen on display at Abergavenny museum.

44. Are there any readers of this Abergavenny book who can recall the whereabouts of this shop 'Star Supply Stores' in the town? It was of course at 11 High Street and these days the premises are occupied by Messrs Stead and Simpson, shoe retailer.

45. High Street in the 1900s, showing the Lipton delivery cart outside the receiving office for the L & N W R parcels. On the left is Bracegirdles, drapers of 23 High Street. On the right hand side, the Victoria Temperance Hotel offers accommodation for tourists and cyclists.

46. Llanfoist brewery seen in this photograph is listed as being run in 1834, by a Mr James Jones. By 1900 it was run by Charles Edwards and was still in business in 1937. The old brewery holds many childhood memories for me, as when we were children, the place was in ruins and we used to climb over the wall and smash all the empty bottles. It seems ironic that now, most of my leisure time is spent travelling around the country collecting them! Today this is the site of the Mountain View housing estate.

LLANFOIST TABLE WATERS LTD.
'Phone : ABERGAVENNY 158.

PRICE LIST

Per Dozen Bottles	26-oz	10-oz	7-oz
CARBONATED DRINKS: Lemonade Orangeade Limeade Raspberryade	3/6d.	2/8d.	2/2d.
GINGER BEER	—	2/8d.	—
SPARKLING DRINKS: Lemon Orange Grapefruit	---	4/0d.	3/0d.
DRY GINGER ALE	—	—	2/2d.
INDIAN TONIC WATER ...	—	—	2/2d.
CONCENTRATED SQUASHES: Lemon Orange Grapefruit Lime Juice	21/6d.	—	—

SODA WATER (40-oz. Syphons)	8/0d. per doz.
CASES charged at	3/0d. per doz.
BOTTLES charged at	2/0d. per doz.
SYPHONS charged at	2/6d. each.

47. On the left is the reverse of the above card showing the tariff of the Llanfoist Table Waters Ltd.

Below is an advert for Eleanor (Powis) Salon, taken from a 1958 guide book.

Phone: 678

Eleanor (Powis) Salon

LADIES HAIR STYLIST		CHILDREN'S HAIR STYLES
PERMANENT WAVING		A SPECIALITY

Town Hall Buildings, Abergavenny

48. The shop founder, Mr Basil Jones and his two sons John and Gerry, outside the shop that has not changed throughout most of this century. After the recent death of Mr Gerry Jones, the last in the family line, Abergavenny museum purchased the shop contents and is in the process of turning it into a display. Today 58 Cross Street is the establishment of Nursery Thymes Babywear shop.

49. Masters, the Cardiff clothiers, owned shops all over Wales. This one at 70 Frogmore Street Abergavenny now houses the offices of the Principality Building Society.

ESTABLISHED 1874.

Post Office Telephone:
No. 11.

Telegrams:
"Thomas, Builder, Abergavenny."

J. G. THOMAS & SONS

BUILDERS, DECORATORS, &c.

HOT & COLD WATER FITTERS,

Offices & Workshops: LION STREET, ABERGAVENNY.

Photo by Eddie Madge

DEPARTMENTS...

High-class Decorating.
Fittings for Churches, Chapels, Clubs.
Shop Fronts and Interiors.
Conservatories.   Greenhouses.
Tiling.   Plastering.
Slating.   Colouring.
Sanitary Plumbing.
Hot-Water Fitting.

SPECIAL ATTENTION
GIVEN TO
LAYING-IN DRAIN
SERVICES WITH THE
LATEST APPROVED
SANITARY FITTINGS.

38

50. Although this is now the car park for the Safeways superstore, J G Thomas and Sons still have an office in Abergavenny situated in Lewis's Lane.

51. Two boxers standing in front of Redwood baker's delivery cart. Probably taken in the Byfield Lane/Tudor Street area, as Redwoods had a bakehouse at 4 Flannel Street and there was a boxing booth in Byfield Lane. The manager of Redwoods was also a keen boxing fan.

52. Outside the Horse and Jockey near Pontypool we can see the delivery cart of Goff Morgan, furniture broker and dealer who had premises at 21 Tudor Street. As a bit of an entrepreneur he also ran the Old Cross Keys public house 41 Tudor Street and also rented out apartments at no. 48.

53. The people shown on this photograph are described on the back of the original postcard, posted on the 2nd September 1905, as the 'rough crew'. The picture is of Mr Samuel Henry Facey with his 'rough crew' outside the Elms, Belmont Road. Mr Facey ran the brewery in Market Street. On March 29th 1899, Facey's supplied the Panteg Hotel with 3 dozen bottles of J J & Sons Whisky for £3/14/0d and 3 cartons of cigarettes at £1/0/0d, a fine example of what a century's inflation has done!

54. The reverse of this card states that this is the staff of Edgar Allen in 1920. In 1895 C J and W Edgar Allen had premises at 69 Frogmore Street. By 1906, it was Allen and Co. Frederick Ball, the insurance agents, took over the premises in the 1920s.

55.   A fine display of pheasants at the premises of Albert Richard Williams of 11 Cross Street. Today
it is a branch of the Cheltenham and Gloucester Building Society, which opened for business in 1971.

56.   A little further along Cross Street is number 6, the premises of Allcott and Co, ironmongers and
cycle accessories vendors. By 1923 it was Allcott and Wilson, and in present times is to be recognised
as the Victoria Wine Store.

57. Number 14 Frogmore Street as it was more than 90 years ago. This was the Old White Horse Inn and the then landlord was Mr Jenkin Williams. Some later landlords who may be remembered were S C S Baker and Ben Evans. Number 14 is no longer a public house and will be better known today as the gents outfitters run by Mr Ian Pountney.

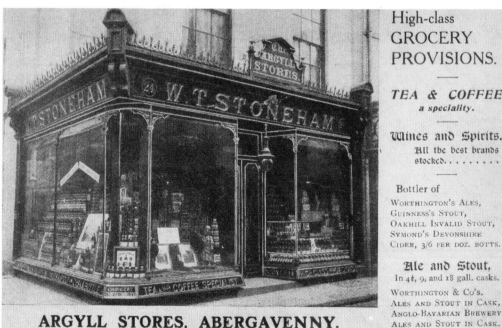

High-class
GROCERY
PROVISIONS.

TEA & COFFEE
a speciality.

Wines and Spirits.
All the best brands stocked. . . . .

Bottler of
Worthington's Ales,
Guinness's Stout,
Oakhill Invalid Stout,
Symond's Devonshire
Cider, 3/6 per doz. botts.

Ale and Stout,
In 4½, 9, and 18 gall. casks.

Worthington & Co's.
Ales and Stout in Cask,
Anglo-Bavarian Brewery
Ales and Stout in Cask.

ARGYLL STORES, ABERGAVENNY.
TELEPHONE: P.O. 32.

58. The shop front of William Thomas Stoneham at No. 24 High Street. Stoneham took over the business from Mr Samuel Pegler in the late 1890s. Prior to this Mr Pegler was in partnership with a Mr William Davis at their grocery shop in Cross Street. No. 24 High Street today, is owned by Messers Dunn & Co.

59. There were a number of George Hotels in Abergavenny at various times and different locations. This one is where you would find Richards Stores today. In 1900, it was run by Mr Denner, who also had a butchery business. By 1923 it was run by Jasper McGeever. Although the shop has seen numerous changes since this early photograph, the building may still be easily recognised by the upper floor windows which remain to this day.

60. John Lawson was the local manager of Eastmans in the 1900s. They also had premises at 67 Frogmore Street. The street numbers altered in the 1920s and 67 became 64 and today number 24 is the premises of Moira's.

H. J. Edwards,

Photo by Eddie Madge.

No. 1, Flannel Street, ABERGAVENNY.

61. These days the business is run by Neil Powell from the same premises. Neil also has a branch in Widemarch Street, Hereford and a wholesale business in Ewyas Harold.

62. This card seems to reflect the many public houses which were in the town in the early part of the 20th century. Novelty postcards were printed in large numbers with the place name left blank, so that local stationers could stamp in the names of the various towns. Here is an example from Abergavenny.

CHAPTER 3

Historic Buildings

63. A view of St Mary's Church from Monk Street in the winter of 1905. St Mary's is one of the largest parish churches in Wales and was originally founded in the year 1090 by the Norman conqueror Hamelin De Ballon.

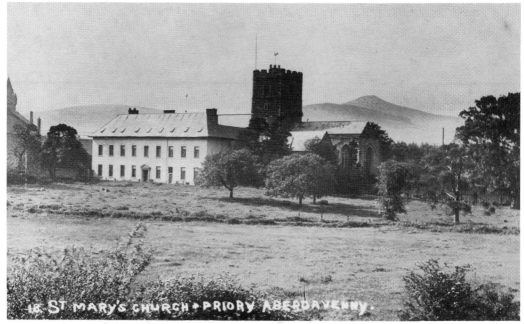

64. The Priory was granted to James Gunter and his brother-in-law Henry Westcott, in 1546. By 1822-23 it was being used as a school for young ladies and by the early 20th century transformed into an hotel. During the 2nd World War it was used as a billet for American troops and was eventually completely demolished in 1952.

65. The Prior's seat and choir stalls which, over the centuries, have suffered all sorts of graffiti. Now, because of the age of some of this, it has itself become part of the church's history. At the time of publication there is a vigorous restoration fund in progress concerning the ancient monuments that adorn St Mary's. The following four photographs show a number of the medieval effigies, some of which date from the 13th century. Sadly, many of these sculptures of oak, alabaster and stone are now showing signs of decay and are in urgent need of repair, with a figure of some £250,000 being quoted as an eventual cost. The fund which was started in 1992 has made good progress and has reached approximately £100,000 but much has yet to be done to preserve these treasures and readers of this Abergavenny book are invited to make a contribution, however small, whenever they see the opportunity.

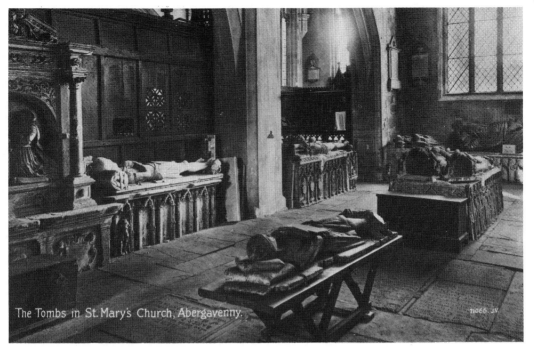

66.   An internal view of the Herbert Chapel of St Mary's with its numerous tombs as photographed almost 100 years ago.

67.   Sir Richard Herbert of Ewyas (died 1510). He was the illegitimate son of Sir William Herbert, the Earl of Pembroke. There is no evidence that he was ever knighted or of him having anything to do with Ewyas. It is thought that these titles were added in the 17th century by his descendants in order to enhance their own pedigree.

41

68. Sir William Ap Thomas who died in 1446 and his wife Gwladys who died in 1454. Sir William was the first of the Herbert family to settle at Raglan. He was the father of William Herbert, 1st Earl of Pembroke.

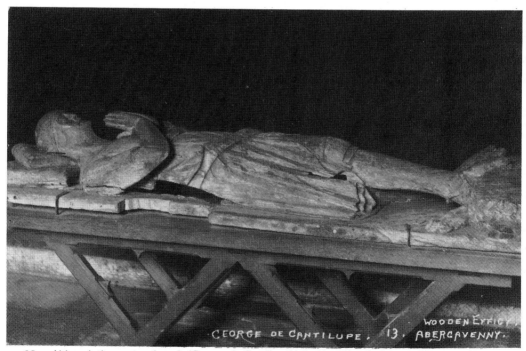

69. Although the postcard reads 'George de Cantilupe' it is thought to be John de Hastings. He was the 11th Lord of Abergavenny who died in 1324.

Holy Trinity Church, Abergavenny   H. Clayton, Monmouth

70. Holy Trinity Church as seen from the Baker Street entrance, was consecrated by the Bishop of Llandaff and Dean of St Paul's, Dr Coplestone, in 1840. It was enlarged, reseated and greatly improved in 1885. Later, in 1897 Miss Rachel Herbert, of Little Mill House, endowed the building of the south aisle; the almshouses and church hall (which started as Trinity School).

71. The church of our Lady's and St Michael's at Pen-y-Pound which was built in 1870. There were two other catholic churches in Frogmore Street before this church was constructed.

Frogmore Street Baptist Chapel   Abergavenny

72.   The Baptist Chapel in Frogmore Street was built in 1878, 50 years after the Baptist church in Market Street and seated up to 700 people. This picture also shows an early view up Pen-y-pound where the Presbyterian church was to be built between 1906-08.

Abergavenny Cemetery

73.   The new cemetery of about 15 acres, was opened in 1894 in the parish of Llanfoist to serve the parishes of Abergavenny, urban and rural.

74. An interesting photograph showing the Deri and Skirrid mountains. Here, in the centre, just in front of the cemetery, can be seen Abergavenny Borough and Abergavenny Rural District Joint Sanatorium Hospital, or the Isolation Hospital as it was also known.

75. The Cottage Hospital on the Hereford Road which was opened in 1902. Before that, it was at 50 Castle Street, with 6 surgeons, 1 dentist and 1 matron. By 1923 it was run by the Joint Hospital Committee, who held their quarterly meetings at the town hall. In 1932, a new maternity wing was opened by the Duke and Duchess of York.

76. In 1884, Nevill Hall was known as the Brooks and belonged to a member of the Vaughan family. By 1901 it was the private residence of the Marquis of Abergavenny who also resided at 64 Ecclestone Square and the Carlton Club, London.

77. In September 1916, the sale of interesting 'freehold, manorial, agricultural and sporting properties, forming a portion of Abergavenny Monmouthshire Estates, belonging to the late Marquis of Abergavenny' (including Nevill Hall) took place. Nevill Hall was purchased by the Blaina Hospital Fund.

78. Another interesting listing from Kelly's directory, this time 1937. R H Stevens ran his catering business from the hall after moving from the castle grounds. Although he published a few postcards from the castle, there does not seem to be any evidence that he continued from here.

79. A rear view of Nevill Hall which many people miss today. The building is now a conference centre and social club.

80. The castle keep was built by the Marquis of Abergavenny as a weekend residence and hunting lodge before he bought the 'Brooks' from the Vaughan family. The Baker-Gabbs, lived in it and maintained it for him. In 1937, R W Thompson states in his book 'An Englishman looks at Wales,' that the ex Mayor, Mr Max Beverage, offered him the castle keep at an annual rent of £50 per year.

Abergavenny Castle

81. A postcard showing the bandstand in the castle grounds, where the town band used to play in order to entertain visitors on weekends and bank holidays.

82. Early this century, a wooden platform formed a walkway all around the castle. There was also a wooden bandstand and it was very popular with visitors who could also purchase refreshments from the tea rooms.

83. In the left hand corner of this picture are the tea rooms in the castle grounds. In 1901, Samuel Davies ran the refreshment rooms at this Abergavenny stronghold. By 1934, Richard Henry Stevens moved his catering business to the castle.

84. Construction of this retreat commenced in 1847. It was known as the Joint Counties Lunatic Asylum and came about because of an agreement between the counties of Hereford, Monmouth Radnor and Brecon. It was opened in 1851 and in 1897 it became the Monmouthshire Asylum.

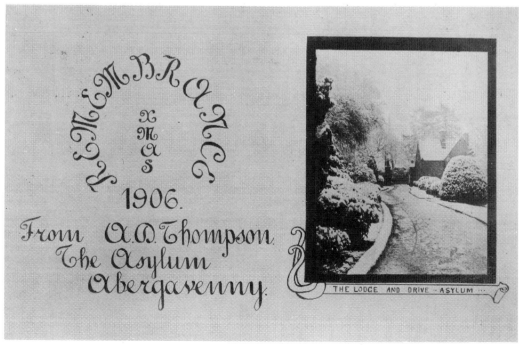

85. A Christmas postcard from the Asylum in 1906, showing the lodge. This is one of a series of postcards showing the Asylum in the early part of this century.

Pen-y-Val. Hospital Abergavenny.

86. A panoramic view of Pen-y-Val, showing the extent of the buildings. The front of this aerial photo would now show the housing estate that has recently been built there. As this Abergavenny book goes to print, Gwent Commission's mental health plans are to close Pen-y-Val completely by March 1996.

87. In 1901 Mandiff Court was the property of Mrs Curre of Itton Court and the home of Col Robert Henry Mansel DL, J P. By 1923 this was unoccupied, but in 1924 it was presented to the Monmouthshire Asylum committee, by Sir John W Beynon Bart CBE DL JL. One of its more noted patients was Rudolf Hess, deputy to Adolf Hitler. Hess, having landed in Scotland in 1941 suing for peace, was interred at Maindiff Court before spending the rest of his days in Spandau prison, Berlin. During periods of relaxation under obvious close supervision, he was allowed to drink at the Victoria Hotel. Maindiff Court was also the home of Crawshay Bailey in the 1870s.

88. A night-time photograph of the former Cottage Hospital which appears to be decorated for a rather special occasion. Opened originally in 1902 as a 'mini hospital' for the treatment of non-infectious diseases and accidents, the building has now been converted into warden controlled accommodation.

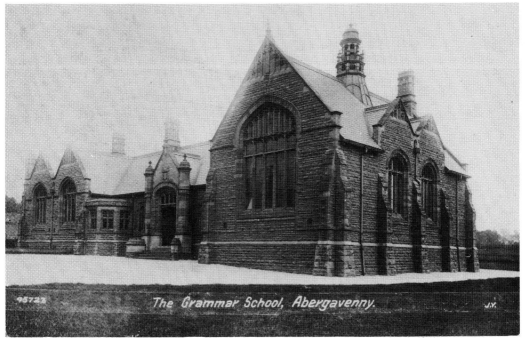

The Grammar School, Abergavenny.

89. The grammar school building in Pen-y-pound, which now houses the careers office and Gwent Theatre, was built in 1898. King Henry VIII Grammar School was founded in Abergavenny in 1543. In 1903, a fee of 7½ or 9 guineas per annum was charged for tuition. This rose to 42 guineas for tuition, board and laundress. Earlier generations will of course recognise a guinea as being worth £1.05.

Girls Intermediate School, Abergavenny.

90. The Girls Intermediate School was established after the Welsh Intermediate Education Act of 1889 and was built in 1897-98. It had an average attendance of 80 and in 1901, Mrs Houlston was the schoolmistress.

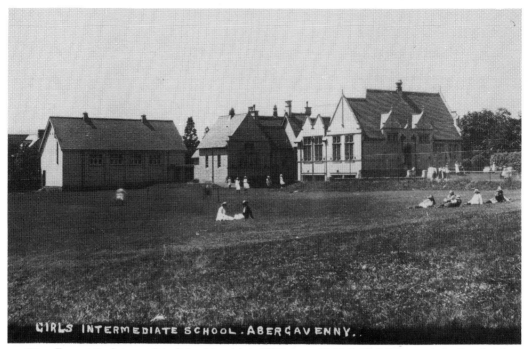

91. Fees at the Intermediate School for girls in 1903, were £1-11-6, £1-3-0 for music (optional) and 7s 6d for gymnastics. It later became Grofield Girls School. Today it is Harold Road Junior School, whose Headmaster, Mr Ken Hewitt, is a committee member of the Welsh Rugby Union.

Bella Vista, Abergavenny.

92. Bella Vista on the Monmouth Road, the home of Mr and Mrs Edwin Foster. Mr Foster was an architect and surveyor in the town. By 1923 he had also been made a Justice of the Peace.

St. Michael's Convent, Abergavenny, Mon. Outside View of the Convent.

93. Here is the convent in Pen-y-Pound before the extensions had been added. This postcard was sent on May 17th 1934 and is written in French, by one of the girls from the convent, showing the teachings of the French Sisters who taught there.

St. Michael's Convent, Abergavenny, Mon. Cricket.

94. Another postcard sent by the same pupil, showing the unusual event of girls playing cricket. In 1920, the convent was run by the sisters of the Holy Ghost with the Rev. Mother Theresa as the superioress.

95. Situated on the Monmouth Road, the impressive Cae Kenfy started the century as the home of a Mrs Batt. William Henry Routledge, J P, was in residence in 1923.

96. Further evidence of late 19th century opulence in Abergavenny is this fine building 'The Beeches', Pen-y-Pound. The picture seen here was taken in 1901 when it was occupied by a Mr Edgar Charles Morgan.

97. Triley Court was once the home of Major E A Sanford, J P. Today it belongs to the Rosenburg Organisation and is a nursing home.

98. Mr Isaac George, J P outside the Manor House, Llanvihangel Gobion. As well as the Manor House he also owned a residence at Mountain Ash called the 'Grove'. He was on the National Eisteddfod Committee in 1913.

99. Trewyn was built in 1695. In 1901 it was the seat of Phillip Bartholomew Barneby Esq B A who, along with Charles Landow, were Lords of the Manor and principal landowners. By 1923 it was unoccupied but by 1934, Mr Constance C Molyneux was in residence. After plans to convert Trewyn into a nursing home failed to materialise, it has been retained as a private dwelling.

100. In 1901 Coldbrook Park was the abode of Arthur Herbert J P. By 1923 he seems to have started a military career for he is listed as Capt Herbert. By 1934 he had been promoted to Major and, after the sale of the Marquis of Abergavenny's estates, he became principal landowner of the area. The premises have since been demolished.

101. A group of army cadets with family and staff outside Llanvihangel Court. Although in 1901, Col George Napier Stuart R E, J P was in residence, it was the property of Harley Rodney Esq. He was, with Jeremiah Lilburn Rosher, a principal landowner in the area.

102. The Gorsedd Circle above, is situated at the Grove, Monmouth Road, where it can still be seen today. This postcard was photographed and published by W J Maidment.

103. This is the impressive War Memorial of Abergavenny, situated in the now very busy thoroughfare of Frogmore Street. It was originally erected to honour those warriors of the district who lost their lives in the Great War of 1914-18. The abundance of wreaths and floral tributes seen here suggests that the photograph was taken at the unveiling ceremony on 29th October 1921 performed by the Lord Lieutenant of the County, Lord Treowen.

Following the 1939-45 conflict an inscription was added to those who gave their lives during the second world war.

104. New colours handed to the 3rd Battalion of the Monmouthshire Regiment, by his Majesty King Edward VII on the 19th June 1909. The 3rd Battalion of the Monmouthshire Regiment consisted mainly of men from Abergavenny and the surrounding area. Because of casualties, they were later amalgamated with the 2nd Monmouthshire Battalion during the 1st World War.

CHAPTER 4

Transport Around Abergavenny

105.   This open-decked bus belonging to the Great Western Railway is full with passengers outside the Bear Hotel in Crickhowell. This modern motorised road transport of the early 1900s seems to have attracted the children to the street to pose for the photographer!

Abergavenny as a Railway Centre

Abergavenny was a vast railway centre during the early part of this century with three stations and goods yards. But after the great depression of the 1930s and with the closure of the steelworks and collieries, the area's rail traffic diminished.

106.   Abergavenny G W R Station (Later Monmouth Road). This station was the first station opened by the Newport, Abergavenny and Hereford Railway Company on the 2nd January 1854. The name Monmouth Road was added in 1950 but was dropped again in 1968 when all the other stations were closed.

107.   This photograph shows the troops preparing to leave the G W R Station during the First World War. They are standing in front of the goods yard which closed in April 1981.

108.   An unusual view of Monmouth Road Station taken from the bridge showing some platform roof renovation in progress.

109.   Abergavenny Junction Station (Ross Road).
This was the only station in the country to be used by both G W R and L M S Railway Companies. Abergavenny Junction Station closed completely on the 9th June 1958 when passenger services were withdrawn. The line itself however, from the junction to Brecon Road was kept open for goods traffic until the 5th April 1971.

HOLY MOUNTAIN ABERGAVENNY.

110. From this old postcard of the Holy Mountain, can be seen the railway carriage sheds which were added to the Junction Station in the early 1920s.

111. An early photograph showing the staff of Abergavenny Junction Station standing on the footbridge. Looking carefully, particularly railway enthusiasts, readers will be able to identify the initials L & N W R on the cap badges thus dating the photograph pre 1923 when the London, Midland and Scottish Railway assumed control.

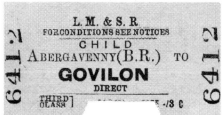

112. Llanvihangel, this is an early photograph showing the three members of staff on the station platform, with the bridge taking the old Hereford road over the railway line behind them. Like numerous other rural stations on the Newport to Hereford line, Llanvihangel closed for passenger traffic on 9th June 1958.

113. A train arriving at Pandy station with only two passengers to pick up. Note the signal box in the background. Well known Abergavenny author Raymond Williams' father was signalman at this station.

114. Penpergwm. Yet another victim of Dr Beeching's railway rationalisation was Penpergwm Station. Here, the photographer catches a steam train approaching the station and its level crossing.

115. From Gilwern there are two more stops before reaching Brynmawr. This is a view of Clydach Station which also shows the tunnels under the Dinas. From Govilon to Brynmawr the railway line tried to follow Bailey's Tramroad but where the tunnels were built the tram road was too sharply curved to follow. On the other side of the Dinas Tunnels was Clydach Halt or Gelli Felen.

116. From Brecon Road Station trains crossed the River Usk, travelling through Llanfoist to Govilon. In 1957, just before passenger services ended, a child's third class ticket from Abergavenny Brecon Road to Govilon direct, would have cost 3d. Three miles before one reached Govilon station, the gradient was found to be 1:34. From Govilon to Brynmawr, for a distance of 5 miles, the gradient was found to vary between 1:37 to 1:40!

117. The rather lonely looking platforms of Gilwern station with a train approaching. This photograph and the one above of Govilon, is the work of pre-war Gilwern photographer Mr F Temple.

118.   The Abergavenny to Merthyr Line. The Abergavenny Junction to Brynmawr line was opened on the 29th September 1862. The Brecon Road goods station remained open until 5th April 1971 but the passenger and through goods services ceased on the 5th January 1958. An early 1/- (5p) return ticket from Abergavenny Junction Station would call at: Abergavenny Brecon Road; Govilon; Gilwern Halt; Clydach; Gelli Felen (Clydach Halt); Brynmawr; Beaufort; Ebbw Vale; Trefil Halt; Nantybwch; Sirhowy; Tredegar; Rhymney Bridge; Dowlais High Street; Pantysgallog Halt; Pontsarn; Cefn Coed; Heolgerrig Halt and Merthyr stations.
These were all pleasant little stations on a picturesque journey of days gone by.

LONDON AND NORTH WESTERN RAILWAY.

POST CARD

Buy the
L. & N. W. Series
of Pictorial
Postcards.

Summer Holiday Excursions for 8 or 15 days.

sets of
different cards.
Over 8 millions

Every FRIDAY, July 7th to September 29th (inclusive).

Finest trains and boats in the world. The L. & N.W.
Railway Company ran special non-stop trains from
London (Euston) to the Riverside Station, Liverpool, in
connection with the sailing of the Atlantic Liners.
Similar arrangements apply in the reverse direction.

TO LIVERPOOL & MANCHESTER DISTRICTS.
NORTH WALES. ENGLISH LAKE DISTRICT.
NORTH EAST COAST RESORTS.
BLACKPOOL.   DOUGLAS (ISLE OF MAN).

ETC., ETC., ETC.

For Fares, Times and full particulars apply at the Stations or to Mr. J. A.
FINDLAY, District Traffic Superintendent, Brecon Road Station, Abergavenny.

McCorquodale & Co., Limited

Brecon Road Station was an important district office as this advertisement states:
'For fares and information apply to Mr J A Finlay, District Traffic Superintendent.

119. Brecon Road Station and Sheds. In its heyday Brecon Road had 12 roads and would have held 100 tank engines easily. By 1933 there were only 46 engines on shed. The through goods services ended on Saturday the 4th January 1958, although there was a special Stephensons Locomotive Society train on Sunday the 5th January 1958.

120. An early photograph of Brecon Road station just in the background, with railway workers carrying out repairs to the bridge over Chapel Road. This bridge no longer exists.

121. A London and North Western Railway delivery cart outside Brecon Road Station. A poster on the side advertises Llandudno as a holiday resort.

122. A group photograph of L & N W R workers from the Brecon Road Station Abergavenny, carrying out repairs on the line at Cwm Felin Fach.

123. Two cards from a collection owned by the Sentinel Truck Company. These cards were kept by the company as a record in case a customer wished to re-order a truck. The first card shows an early steam powered vehicle belonging to W Whiting, Contractor, Abergavenny. It was photographed outside the Sentinel Factory.

124. Another truck supplied by Sentinel to Whiting's. This time on the back of the card are the following details which might be of interest to the commercial vehicle enthusiast:-
Engine - 6 cyls developing 60 DLP at 3000 RPM Coil ignition. Petrol Tank - 18 gals mounted on offside. S V electric pressure pump. Wheel base - 10ft /0 1/2 in R A Ratio - 7:1 Bodywork - 11ft long 6ft 8 ins wide. Lined steel throughout. 18 ins hinged sides and tailboard. Bracing chains fitted. Tipping gear - Bromilon and Edwards under type. Power operated. Twin Ram hydraulic. 3 way. Frame pressed steel channels. Unladen weight - Under 3 tons. Legal Speed -20 MPH. Annual Tax - £35 List Price - £543 approx.

125. An early Red and White single decker bus with crew outside Abergavenny Motors, which is now the premises of A.T.S. and Abergavenny Renault. Most of the Red and White buses were manufactured by the Albion Company but this bus is a PLSC Leyland and could well have belonged to a private operator before the Red and White takeover.

126. Another of the Sentinel trucks, this time belonging to the Williams brothers. Note the rather ancient telephone number on the side of the vehicle which takes us back a few years!

Photo—Saltinstall, Abergavenny.

Mr. Edwin Prosser and his Bi-plane,
Abergavenny, September 6th, 1913.

Preparing for a Flight.

127./128. The first demonstration of flying at Abergavenny was given by a Mr Radley of Bedford in 1910 with his monoplane or 'Flying Machine' as aircraft were then called. A crowd of some 6000 people thronged Bailey Park to witness the event which unfortunately did not last too long. The pilot apparently misjudged his landing and crashed into the park railings causing much damage to his machine, but managing to survive himself. Both of these photographs show a display some three years later by a Mr Edwin Prosser, this time with a more advanced Biplane type of craft.

Photo—Saltinstall, Abergavenny.

Mr. Edwin Prosser and his Bi-plane,
Abergavenny, September 6th, 1913.

End of a Flight—Planing Down.

129. Newport photographers Williams, Ware and Curnik, published this photograph of the G W R omnibus passing the Swan Hotel. As there was no railway line to Brecon from Abergavenny, G W R operated a bus service from Monmouth Road railway station to the square in Brecon. Below is a ticket from this bus.

130. An advertisement from Bevan's appears on one side of ticket and on the other is a list of all the 16 stops which the bus made.

131. This unusual photograph may be of particular interest to commercial vehicle enthusiasts. It shows three steam powered trucks belonging to Tim Price of Llanover, all linked together attempting to haul a large container to the site of a reservoir under construction at Talybont.

132. A railwayman's union outing of some years ago. The trippers are posing alongside the charabanc outside the Somerset Public House in Merthyr Road.

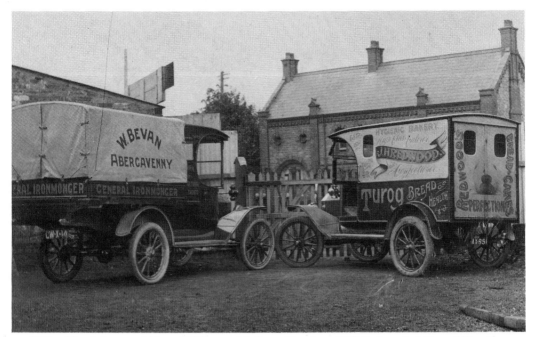

133. The delivery vehicles of W Bevan, 10 Cross Street, and J H Redwood, 4 Flannel Street are parked in a compound opposite the drill hall in Baker Street. The house to house delivery of bread has all but disappeared unfortunately and how many readers can recall 'Turog' bread as advertised on the side of the van?

134. An open topped double decker bus travelling down Frogmore Street. The bus was a Milnes Daimler belonging to the G W R.

135. On the left of this picture can be seen the George Hotel where Richards' store is today. On the opposite side, next to the Herefordshire House, is Morgan's the stationers who published the Abergavenny Chronicle. Note the line of carriages parked outside the cab stand. This is where the War memorial is today.

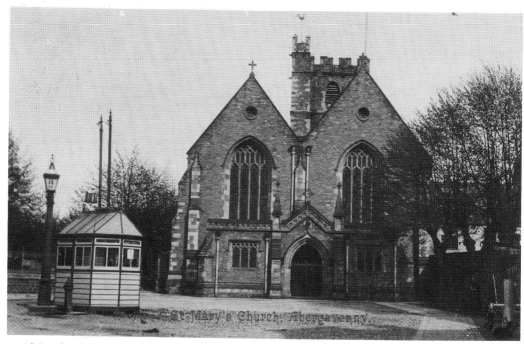

136. Another cab stand, this time outside St Mary's Church. There were two cab proprietors listed as operating in Abergavenny in 1901. They were George H Bradley of Ross Road and Richard Powis of 2 Merthyr Road. These two were still operating in 1923 but Richard was now in business with his brother trading under the name of Powis Brothers, Brecon Road.

CHAPTER 5

Events & Momentous Occasions

137. National Eisteddfod, Abergavenny. August 4th-9th 1913. On July 3rd 1912, it was announced that Abergavenny would host the National Eisteddfod. This card is a souvenir proclamation and various committees were set up to organise the event. Below is a list of some of the chief committee members as taken from the souvenir programme. It reads as a 'Who's who' of the district at that time.

Executive Committee Chairman Major General Sir Ivor Herbert Bart C.B. C.M.G. M.P. Llanarth. Vice Chairman Alderman J Straker, Mayor, J.P. C.C. Abergavenny. Hon Sec R H Jackson, Fernlea, Hereford Road, Abergavenny.
Finance Committee Chairman Mr D Howell James, National Provincial Bank, Abergavenny.
Literary Committee Chairman Colonel J A Bradney, Talycoed, Abergavenny.
Art, Science and Industry Committee Chairman Rt Hon Lady Llangattock, The Hendre.
Pavilion Committee Chairman Mr Isaac George, J.P. Manor House, Llanvihangel Gobion.
Advertising, Printing and Bill Posting Committee Chairman Mr J R Jacob, Solicitor, Lion Street, Abergavenny.
Railway Arrangements and Accommodation Committee Chairman Alderman J G Bishop, Avenue Road, Abergavenny.

138. On this souvenir postcard can be seen a small photograph of the Eisteddfod pavilion. This was erected by Messrs Foster and Hill, Contractors, Abergavenny, and was decorated by Mr C Downes, Furnishers, Frogmore Street. The plan for the Eisteddfod was drawn up by Mr B J Francis of Abergavenny. In the souvenir programme it is stated that the marquee be auctioned by James Straker, Sons and Chadwick (partners William Chadwick and Charles Straker) on Thursday, August 28th at 2:00pm. If you had a reserved season ticket, it would have cost thirty shillings (£1.50). This would have entitled you to four Eisteddfod meetings, five concerts (transferable) and to pass in and out of the park. An ordinary season ticket with reserved seats would have cost twenty shillings (£1.00) and would have entitled you to four meetings and five concerts.

139. The Pageant of Gwent. On the first day of the Eisteddfod, the Pageant of Gwent was held at Maindiff Court. The date of this was Monday 4th August 1913 and proceedings began at 2:30pm. 800 characters took part. There were 12 episodes, including the History of the Eisteddfod, Leaders of Gwent from the coming of Cwmry to the reign of Charles I.

140. Harry Shackleton was the official photographer and he took all the photographs of the Pageant and this is just one of the many scenes from the event that were published by him.

141. Above, members of the Pageant of Gwent in the National Eisteddfod procession. Although the Eisteddfod started on Bank Holiday Monday, the actual Eisteddfod procession did not take place until Tuesday at 8:00am. This commenced at the Town Hall and reached the Grove, Monmouth Road at 8:30am.

142. Above, a postcard posted in 1911, showing the local Eisteddfod taking place in the castle grounds.

143. The Abergavenny Eisteddfod. The Abergavenny Cymreigyddion Society held annual Eisteddfodau as early as 1833. There are several early accounts of these in the Illustrated London News. The society had its own hall in Tudor Street but the printed postcard above shows the event being held in the Market Hall.

ABERGAVENNY CHAIR EISTEDDFOD,
—— EASTER MONDAY, 1908. ——

Priory Road,
Abergavenny.

MY DEAR SIR OR MADAM,
    I beg to remind you that the Entries for the above Eisteddfod close as follows :—
    Choral Events, 23rd March, 1908.
    Band Contest, 23rd March, 1908.
    Solo Classes, 6th April, 1908.
    Literature & Art Events, 6th April, 1908.
and sincerely trust you will be in a position to forward entry form completed before these dates.
    Should you require further entry forms or additional information of any kind, I shall be delighted to supply same.
        Yours sincerely,
          R. H. JACKSON.

144. This card was used by the secretary of the society, Mr R H Jackson to advertise the event in 1908 and this is the reverse side. A total of £300 worth of prizes was being offered, a grand sum indeed for the period when an average weekly wage in the district was less than £2!

145. The official opening of the new part of the Abergavenny Cattle Market. Lord Waldegrave is outside the main entrance of the sale ring, on December 16th 1958.

146. A general view of part of the cattle market on the same day, showing the main ring, sales ring, canteen and offices.

147. The foundation stone for the library was laid in 1905. Andrew Carnegie, the benefactor, was invited to perform the ceremony but was otherwise engaged. He was also invited to open the building officially , but again declined, although his signature does appear in the visitors book at a later date.

148. The procession arriving at the library for the official opening, on Sunday 8th September 1906. The sign on the door reads, 'No dogs or bicycles allowed, By order.'

149.   On this postcard, someone has pointed out the Lord Mayor of London leaving the library after his official opening duties. They also indicated that the two statues either side of the doorway are of Andrew Carnegie and The Marquis of Abergavenny.

150.   Sir Walter Vaughan Morgan, the Lord Mayor of London, and his party at the public reception for him in the town hall.

151. Following the reception, as pictured on the previous page, the visitors attended Bailey Park for a military tournament. Along with the Lord Mayor of London's party, are G Watkin, the Mayor of Abergavenny and his guests. On the 10th September the Mayor received the freedom of the Borough of Abergavenny.

152. To commemorate the visit, The Lord Mayor was asked to plant an avenue of trees through Bailey Park, which are still there to this day.

153. Earl Roberts arriving for the public luncheon at the town hall. He is seen walking in front of, what is today, the council offices. Earl Roberts (1832-1914) was the distinguished military leader of the late 19th century and was to become Commander in Chief of the British Army, accomplishing the great victories of Afghanistan and South Africa. The Earl commanded worldwide admiration for his achievements, thus it was that the population of Abergavenny paid such great regard to the visit of such an important figure to the town.

154. Leaving the town hall after the public luncheon. The large crowd blocking Market Street are watching the Earl leave to go to Bailey Park.

155. The procession from the town hall with the town councillors arriving at St Mary's Church. Note the lamp post by the cab stand on the left. A large crowd has gathered and the shopkeepers have certainly made an effort with the decorations.

156. This is the plaque that Earl Roberts unveiled in St Mary's Church on 30th August 1905. It was erected to honour those volunteers of Abergavenny and the district who had served in and lost their lives during the South African War 1899-1902. Following the unveiling ceremony, the Earl was presented with the Freedom of the Borough in recognition of the eminent military services which he had rendered to the British Empire.

157. The public luncheon for Earl Roberts at the town hall with a band ready to play. Bessy Powell, an aunt of past Mayoress Mrs Marion Webb, was present at this function.

158. A 1900 photograph of the laying of the foundation stone of the YMCA building in Frogmore Street. Before this building transpired, the Young Men's Institute used to meet at the National School in Park Street where J H Green was Honorary Secretary. The shop is now occupied by Mr John Bannon, of Jaybee's Soft Furnishings.

159. The Marquis of Abergavenny, seated in the rear of a Ford motorcar with a Mrs Duberley. The driver is a Col. Pearson and the front passenger is Col. Steel. They are testing a trestle bridge built across the river Usk in August 1914. There was an abundance of military training in the district at this time, for war with Germany had just been declared.

160. Another photograph of the same bridge with a full complement of the Royal Engineers stood at ease, to test its sturdiness. This postcard was sent from A Williams of King Street to his sister Mrs L Henry in Port Talbot. What a catastrophe would have occurred had the bridge collapsed, with just one small boat and two lifejackets to be shared amongst almost 100 men.

161. This time a pontoon bridge. There were a number of different bridges built across the River Usk by the military, Abergavenny being regularly used as a training camp. Note the gasometers in the background.

162. A footbridge for troops only, built across the river not far from where the ferry to Govilon used to operate. These bridges must have been built and taken down, each time there was a military camp in Abergavenny.

163. Behind the troops marching up Frogmore Street are the houses which, in 1913, became the Post Office. Today it is the premises of W M Nicholas. Note the gas lamp in the foreground, the street-lighting of the period operated by the Abergavenny Gas Company.

164. The tool cart of the Welsh Engineers. They are seen passing in front of the Kings Arms in Nevill Street, on the 13th August 1908, after having marched up Tudor Street. The poster in the windows of the shop next to the Kings Arms advertises the Tomkin and Chadwick sale in the Market Hall. In 1900 Thomas Harrill Tomkins was an auctioneer at 55 Frogmore Street, he also had premises in Bristol. By 1902, he had taken on William Morgan Chadwick as a partner. By 1920 Chadwick had assumed control of the business and later went into partnership with James Straker. In 1817 the pub was used as a billet for troops of The King's and 15th Hussars who were called into the district in the wake of serious rioting at Nantyglo and Tredegar. They left their mark in the form of graffiti over the fireplace 'Good quartering forever 1817 King & 15 Hussars Hall Troop 24'.

165. A tank named 'Julian', raising money for war bonds outside the former Presbyterian (Whitfield) church hall, where Tesco's is today. The mayor, Zachariah Wheatley, can be seen on top of the tank displaying the amount raised so far. This was one of several tanks which travelled around the country in order to raise money for the war effort, each tank having its own name.

166. With all the flags decorating the streets, and somebody waving the American flag from the town hall, it looks as if this is the celebration of the end of the First World War in 1918.

167. The Duke of Wellington's Regiment, (33rd West Riding), arriving from the Brecon Road Station in 1925. The photo was taken by a Hereford Photographer, Mr A G Price.

168. The Welsh Fusiliers arriving at the LNWR Brecon Road Station in 1909. The railway bridge crossing Chapel Road has long since gone, so too has the house to be seen under the bridge.

169. Another military procession, this time from the GWR Railway Station, Monmouth Road. The photo was taken by R H Stevens whilst he was still based in Crickhowell, around 1903 to 1913.

Printed in England.

POST CARD

THE
L. & N. W. R.
SERIES OF
PICTORIAL
POSTCARDS.

FOR POSTAGE IN THE UNITED KINGDOM ONLY
THIS SPACE MAY BE USED FOR CORRESPONDENCE.

(FOR ADDRESS ONLY.)

MONSTER FÊTE—BAILEY PARK, ABERGAVENNY.

Monday, 16th September, 1907.

THIRD ANNUAL

GRAND MILITARY TOURNAMENT.

Champion Competitors.

Ambulance, Fire Brigade, and Volunteer Competitions.
Steeplechase. - Variety Performances. - Fireworks.

Admission 6d. Children 3d.

CHEAP BOOKINGS FROM ALL STATIONS

Full particulars from Hon. Sec.—W. LLEWELLIN, Abergavenny.

170. On the reverse of a London North Western Railways postcard, is an advertisement for a Monster Fete in 1907, with a grand military tournament.

171. Abergavenny played host to many military camps in the early part of this century. Here are a few of the many different regiments that visited the district. Also there are many photographers from outside the area who followed the troops here. The regiment is possibly that of the Pioneers at Abergavenny in 1913, waiting for their pay. On another card of this same regiment, posted to a colonel in France, the sender says they had a wonderful camp and spent a lot of time chasing a Welsh rabbit around the mountains 2000 ft above sea level.

172. German prisoners of war being marched down Brecon Road, towards Llanbedr where the prison camp was located. Photographed by R H Stevens of Abergavenny, it is thought that it is his bicycle resting on the railings outside Knoll Cottage.

CHAPTER 6

Sport, Leisure & Entertainment

173. Left, a postcard of the Coliseum picture house in 1913 with the building of the roof still in progress. In 1923 the Abergavenny Coliseum Company Ltd were the proprietors, with Harry Waller Wesley as resident manager. This company went into voluntary liquidation in May 1995.

174. The September fair at what is now the Fairfield car park. This was in 1912, but the traditional fair days still take place today.

175. The Abergavenny Light Opera Company pictured in October 1991 having celebrated a 25th Anniversary production. The performance was of 'La Vie Parisienne' and the cast comprises of; left to right from the back row - Bernard Zavishlock, Unknown, Glyn Heard, Frank Jones, Arthur Small, David Arnold, Geoff Allen, Tom Richards, Cliff Mallet, Harry Wyatt and Keith Purkiss. Second row: Pat Purkiss, Margaret Allen, Margaret Heard, Thelma George, Unknown, Liz Rigby, Betty Withers, Margaret Wyatt, Betty Evans, Katy Morgan, Grace Denbury, Eluned Rolf and Carl Marshall. First row: Paul Jones, Gayner Adams, Jean Evans, Pam Martin, Mary Cummings, Dee McElroy, Adoree Flower, Mary Thomas, Elaine Jones, Sue Williams, Anne Marshall and Randall Evans. Seated: Val Stephens, Tony Paton, Chris Davies, Richard Stephens, Jimmy Murphy, Ivor Lewis, Diane Dawes, Barrie Jackson, Rita Rouse, Gill Crane, Barry Evans and Liz O'Brian. Floor: Jane Lewis, Carol Paton, Sarah Griffin and Sue Price.

176. The stage is set on this occasion for 'Die Fledermaus' in October 1989 and the performers are as follows:- Sam Coles, David Arnold, Geoff Allen, Arthur Smith and Cliff Mallet. Second row: Glyn Heard, Unknown, Tom Richards, Randall Evans, Harry Wyatt, David Evans, Ken Williams, Unknown, Margaret Heard, Marian Jones, Betty Evans, Thelma George, Unknown, Val Stephens, Unknown, Mary Cummings, Unknown, Unknown, Jean Evans, Edwin Rigby, Betty Withers and Grace Denbury. First row: Melanie Davies, Eluned Rolf, Gill Crane, Gayner Adams, Pat Purkins, Jill Williams, Anne Marshall, Unknown, Unknown, Adoree Flower, Katya Morgan, Mary Thomas, Marjory Ballett, Margaret Wyatt, Liz O'Brien, Voyna Harris and Bernard Zavishlock. Seated: Marian Copp, Ivor Lewis, Barrie Jackson, Penny Edwards, Carl Marshall, Dianne Davies, Richard Stephens, Ursula Pomfrey, Carol Walters, Unknown, Pam Martin, Tony Paton, John Davies. Sitting on the floor: Louise Ransom, Sue Price, Sarah Griffin, Chris Davies, Joan Barrie, Penny Martin, Carol Paton, Jane Lewis, Brenda Maloney and Sue Williams.

177. An early look at the interior of the Market Hall. Posing for the cameraman is the cast of the ever popular Gilbert and Sullivan's *Pirates of Penzance*.

178. What appears to be a walking race in progress. The Capital and Counties Bank is in the background, in 1903, the manager was Mr Bretherton. This later became Moon & Co's Garage, then W H Smith and today it is Family Value. In 1825 The White Horse Inn was the starting point for a walking race which involved walking 66 miles a day for 6 days.

179. An early military sports event taking place in Bailey Park. In this postcard, we can clearly make out the pole vault.

180. Probably on the same occasion as mentioned in the previous photograph, is this rather odd event. An action shot with a difference, as one of the soldiers appears to be serving as a pole for a would be vaulter!

POST CARD

THE L. & N. W. R. SERIES OF PICTORIAL POSTCARDS.

FOR POSTAGE IN THE UNITED KINGDOM ONLY
THIS SPACE MAY BE USED FOR CORRESPONDENCE.

(FOR ADDRESS ONLY.)

DON'T FORGET

- - Grand Band Contest, - -

ABERGAVENNY CASTLE—Saturday, 5th October, 1907.

——— MAGNIFICENT PRIZES ———

.. ALSO ..

Great Waltzing Competition, The Novelty .. .. of the Season.

"WALTZING WITH JULIA." No Entrance Fee.

ADMISSION 6d.
Cheap Bookings from all Stations.

Full particulars from Hon. Sec. :—
W. LLEWELLIN,
ABERGAVENNY.

Printed by Metropolitan & Co., Limited.

POST CARD

THE L. & N. W. R. SERIES OF PICTORIAL

Printed in England.

LOOK OUT FOR THE . . **Abergavenny Dog Show,**

To be held in the . . General Market Hall, *6n Thursday, November 21st, 1907.*

Patron - THE MOST HONOURABLE THE MARQUIS OF ABERGAVENNY, K.G.

President—HIS WORSHIP THE MAYOR OF ABERGAVENNY (Councillor W. D. WOODWARD).

—Vice Presidents—

CODRINGTON F. CRAWSHAY, Esq., J.P., C.C.   ALDERMAN JAMES STRAKER, J.P., C.C.
COLONEL BLEDDIAN HERBERT, J.P.   B. W. POWLETT, Esq.
MAYOR J. H. HARRIS, J.P.   D. JONES, Esq., J.P., M.F.H.
J. A. FINDLAY, Esq.   E. PERIE GORDON, Esq., J.P.

Chairman of Committees—B. W. POWLETT, Esq.
Secretary—Mr. C. POWELL, 12, High Street, Abergavenny.
Treasurer—Mr. W. M. CHADWICK, Frogmore Chambers, Abergavenny.

Entries close November 14th, 1907.

Benching and Feeding by "Old Calabar," Liverpool.

CHEAP TICKETS will be issued.

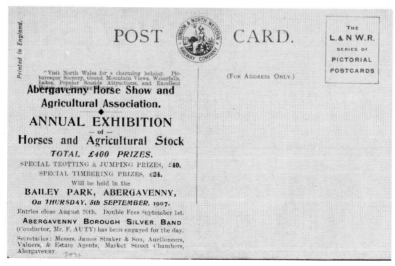

POST CARD.

THE L. & N. W. R. SERIES OF PICTORIAL POSTCARDS

Printed in England.

"Visit North Wales for a charming holiday. Picturesque Scenery, Grand Mountain Views, Waterfalls, Lakes, Popular Seaside Attractions, and Excellent

Abergavenny Horse Show and Agricultural Association.

◆

ANNUAL EXHIBITION
— of —
Horses and Agricultural Stock

TOTAL £400 PRIZES.

SPECIAL TROTTING & JUMPING PRIZES, £40.
SPECIAL TIMBERING PRIZES, £24.

Will be held in the

BAILEY PARK, ABERGAVENNY,

On THURSDAY, 5th SEPTEMBER, 1907.

Entries close August 20th. Double Fees September 1st.

ABERGAVENNY BOROUGH SILVER BAND
(Conductor, Mr. F. AUTY) has been engaged for the day.

Secretaries: Messrs. James Straker & Son, Auctioneers, Valuers, & Estate Agents, Market Street Chambers, Abergavenny.

(FOR ADDRESS ONLY.)

---

181. The reverse of three London and North Western Railway postcards showing adverts for local events in 1907.

182. Hockey began in Abergavenny in about 1897 and in the season 1901-02 the club had an unbeaten Welsh record. The Wales and Ireland International was held in Abergavenny in 1902 and over 100 members paid 37½p per season membership. All the top London and Midlands teams came to Abergavenny on tour. J Jonathon, the father of former Mayor of Abergavenny, Jack Jonathan, is pictured 2nd left standing. He later became a Welsh International.

183. Abergavenny Hockey club 2nd XI Season 1906-07. In 1907, Abergavenny hosted the Wales v Scotland Hockey International which Scotland won 1-0. As well as a first and second team, they hosted a 3rd and a Thursday XI, such was the popularity of the sport at the time.

184. Abergavenny S.A.U.C.C. team season 1910. The author has yet to establish exactly what the initials SAUCC stood for and would welcome information from any readers of this book who may recall such an occasion.

185. The Grammar School XI cricket team circa 1906, along with the sports master with his pipe.

186. Abergavenny RFC's season 1904. Prior to playing their fixtures in Bailey Park, they would play at Stanley Fields on Hereford Road. Before their present clubhouse was built in the Fairfield car park, they changed at what was, the London Hotel on the corner of Monk Street.

187. Gilwern AFC, Season 1912-13, who played in the West Monmouthshire League. They are pictured here with 'Tommy' the team mascot.

188. An interesting postcard showing the River Usk at Llanfoist with men fishing from a boat. Ladies and gentlemen are playing golf on the Monmouthshire golf course and in the background can be seen the stand and rails of the Abergavenny Racecourse, which once held the Welsh Grand National. This fact is mentioned in Reginald Herbert's 'When Diamonds Are Trumps'.

189. One of the many football teams in Abergavenny at the beginning of this century. The photograph was taken by Harry Shackleton.

190. Abergavenny RFC Centenary Season 1974-75. Back row, left to right are C Williams, C Durose, R Howells, A Jones, M Aylett, D Jones, A Thomas, S Davies and E Smith. Middle (standing): P Coleman, W Macpherson, A Price, J Siddons, P Exton, B Thomas, M Houghton, R Lewis, R Morgan, C Macpherson, C Richards, M Schwank, B Clark, N Evans, I Pickford, R Siddons, P Gething, W Griffiths, R James, M Jennings, J Mills and P Lewis. Middle (seated): G Lewis, R Morgan, M Bruton (Capt. 'Quins), K Hewitt (Sec), A W Breeze (Chairman), I Morgan (Capt. 1st XV), P Bruton, L Bannon and K Holley. Front (Youth XV): H Thomas, P Kelly, N Generalovic, R Bennett, G Brown, A Green, I Powell, J Bannon, J Gardner (Capt.), R Davies, C Marlog, H Meats, P Matthews, G Neil, C McCarthy and D Phelps.

107

191. The team of 1994-95 which won promotion to the Heineken League. To be seen left to right, back row are: Mike Aylett (Chairman), Chris Price, Geoff Williams, Robert Harris, Geoff Shackleton, Andrew Sutton, Paul Daniels, Richard Dixon, Ken Walters, Bryan Morgan, Gary Lawrence and Phil Jones (Secretary). Front row: Phil Anstey, Owen Cooper, Carl Walbyoff, Rob McCormack, Mike Williams (Captain), Mark Symons, Geraint Pritchard, Leighton Thomas and Craig Lancaster.

192. King Henry VIII Grammar School 2nd year cricket team in 1969. Back row, left to right: Mr Gwyn Jones (Head of P E), Lyndon Stockham, Chris Hawkins, Stephen Hughes, Paul Carver, Les Nash, David Price and Russell Edwards (Headmaster). Front row: Peter Kelly, John Bannon, Gavin Palmer, Jeff Gardner, Andy Nash and Richard Rossiter.

193. This time it is the turn of the RFC committee to pose for the cameraman during the 1994-95 season. Left to right, back row are: Greg Baker, Mark Neil, Ron Hinksman, Derek Ellis, Ian Jones, Stuart Spencer, Brian Griffiths, Colin Watson, Ian Costin, Brian Baldwin and Phil Webb. Front row: Clive Howells, Chris Breakwell, Gareth Havard, Mike Aylett, Phil Jones, John Townsend and Terry West.

194. An historic event in the rugby world in 1991 and on display is the first World Rugby Cup ball. The match ball for the first world cup was run around Bailey Park by Abergavenny mini rugby players and then on to the Mayor's Parlour. To be seen in this photograph are: Mike Aylett, Rosa Norris, John Powell, Ken Hewitt, John Prince, Terry Vaux, Clive Howells, Chris Padfield, Rees Van-der-Vyver, Joe Bevan and Kristian Merrett.

CHAPTER 7

The Surrounding Villages

195. An early postcard of Govilon showing J Davies, Grocer, which is now the village Post Office. On the right is the Lion Hotel which appears to be receiving a delivery by horse and cart.

196. The remains of the Old Forge, Gilwern, showing the past industrial links with the Clydach Valley. This postcard was photographed in about 1920.

197. Local photographer John Meredith captured this tranquil scene at Forge Row, Gilwern some 70 or 80 years ago. Some villagers stand in the doorway of one of the cottages whilst a lone pig makes its way down the lane.

198. Two views of the main street in Gilwern village. The shop on the left belongs to Jasper Edwin Watkins who was a grocer and baker and next to this is the Post Office. In 1901 Elizabeth Jane Winston was the sub post mistress and advertised as a painter. By 1923 Mary Jane Davies had taken over as both sub post mistress and painter.

199. The same street, this time looking downwards. The man on horseback is outside the Post Office. Edwin John Goodden was the landlord of the Beaufort Arms, who also hired out boats on the canal. Jacob Watkin was Gilwern's own canal inspector. As well as the Beaufort Arms there were three other pubs in Gilwern in 1901. The Lion Inn, The Corn Exchange and the Commercial Stores.

200. Fred Temple was out to photograph Ty Mawr ablaze. E Hunt tells Miss G Hunt, of Field Farm, Overmonnow, 'This is a card of Ty Mawr. I'll send you more later. Please keep them'.

201. This picture was taken on the 17th March 1906. It shows the firefighters posing outside the ruined Ty Mawr building although Mr Temple is using artistic licence by drawing in some flames.

202. Group 4 Govilon School. Although there is no date, the photographer R H Stevens was based in Crickhowell between 1900 and 1910, and of course the young ladies' classroom attire is a good clue as to the age of this traditional school photograph.

203. Govilon AFC of the 1969-70 Season and seen left to right are: Back row, Roy Stockham, Keith Burns, Vernon Lewis, Bas Davies, Alan Stockham and Paul Sussex. Front: Archie Aubry, David Williams, Malcolm Powell, Keith Burns and Paul Williams.

204. The Gilwern Scout Group was formed in 1957 the year of the movement's Golden Jubilee by the Rev. Edgar Powell, their first meetings being held in the vestry of Gilwern Congregational Church. The old Gilwern Station became their next venue in 1960 with several other locations until the completion of their new and permanent headquarters at the playing fields in 1994. The efforts of the group and the many supporters have been more than commendable over the years in achieving their aims of having a 'home of their own'. Seen in this photograph in 1986 of the group five-a-side competition, Gilwern Cub Group winners are: the late Peter Coleman, Mayor of Abergavenny with Kevin Buck. The lads pictured left to right with the trophy are: Ian Worrollo, Jonathan Sturley, Guy Solomon, Stephen Jones and Graham Jones.

205. This is the Scout Camp to Dipple Farm, Bideford in 1988 and pictured left to right are, back row: Martin Reah, Jeremy Simpson, Richard ?, Kevin Bennett, Ian Worrollo, Wayne Back, Stuart Hillman, Toby Griffiths and Gill Buck. Front row: James Daunter, Jonathon Hands, Lachlan Fairgrieve, Andrew Payne and Shaun Buck.

The Boat House, Gilwern 1903

206. One of the Sunday afternoon entertainments, taking a boat trip along the canal circa 1920. Boating on this stretch of the Monmouthshire and Brecon canal has seen a new lease of life in recent years and has now become a favourite attraction to locals and visitors.

Otter hunting on the River Usk at Gilwern

207. There are not many, if any, otters to hunt on the Usk today. Early this century, hunting in general, including otter hunting was very popular in the area.

208. The Brecknock and Abergavenny canal was started from Gilwern to Brecon and was opened on December 24th 1800, but it was not until January 1805, that the section between Gilwern and Llanfoist was completed.

209. An early printed postcard sent in 1909. The sender says that they have arrived from Brynmawr to Gilwern by train and have travelled along the road to Abergavenny, passing through Govilon.

210. The Govilon Tea rooms are now cottages opposite the Bridgend public house.

Llanfoist &
Abergavenny. 670.

211. The school house in the centre of the picture, will give you your bearings. No housing estates in this photograph, with the cutting running along the railway line into Abergavenny.

St Faith's Church Llanfoist. 694

212. St Faith's Church, where 'Welsh only' services were preached until the influx of the English language in about 1850. In 1873, Crawshay Bailey had the church restored in memory of his father who was buried there. The Steel family, notable surgeons, also have several members interred in this graveyard.

213. Significant changes have taken place since this photograph of Llanfoist was taken in about 1920. Particularly of course the disappearance of the railway bridge seen in the background.

214. Quieter days for Llanfoist boathouse, which was built in around 1815. In the early and middle years of the 19th century, coal, iron and limestone were loaded into barges for delivery to Newport and the rest of the world. Today it is the premises of the Beacon Hill Boats, which hire out canal barges for leisure trips.

215. Members of the hunt at Llanellen in the early part of this century. The postcard shows the cottage which is now the Craft Shop. The house in the background has since been demolished.

216. A printed postcard showing the Post Office with Howell Moses, the sub postmaster, his wife and three daughters. He was also a blacksmith.

217. Apart from the appearance of the new road, the houses on the right, have not altered much throughout the century. In 1901 Mrs William Philips ran the Bell public house. By 1920 Thomas Arthur Davis had taken over, who also received GWR parcels at this address. The sub postmaster was Cornelius Pocock.

218. The Mission Church Glangrwyney in about 1920. Llangenny as well as Glangrwyney came under the parish of Llangenau at about this time. There were two bridges over the River Usk in the area, one of which was a toll bridge and the tollgate keeper was Mrs Emily Edwards.

219. The Skirrid Mountain Inn is advertised as the oldest inn, in the country and is said to date back to the year 1111. Still a very popular place to wine and dine to this day, it is situated just a short distance from Abergavenny near the Hereford Road. The picture seen here was taken in about 1915 when Mr Richard Large was the landlord.

220. Llanvihangel Post and Telegram office, circa 1903. The sub-postmaster was Alfred John Watkins. By 1923, he was also the blacksmith. In 1934 William Walton had taken over the Post Office and advertised as a motor engineer instead of a blacksmith.

221. With the speed of modern-day traffic passing through Llanover these days, one would be very unwise to walk in the road. On the left hand side is the Post Office. In 1901, David Jones was the sub postmaster and also a carpenter.

222. The Gwesty Tea Rooms Llanover. On bank holidays, families from the Blaenavon area used to walk over the mountain down to Llanover, where the Gwesty was a favourite stopping place. In 1901 David Davies ran it as a coffee tavern.

223. Llanfoist County Primary School and the pupils here are: Back row, left to right: Mostyn Goodwin, Jane White, Granville Jones, David Jones, Martin Powell, Caroline Mills, Unknown and Jenny Poulson. Middle row: Kay Mills, Denise Hillebrand, Helen Prosser, Julie James, David Isaac, Julie Bannon, Kevin Badham and Peter Payne. Front row: Debbie Harris, Julie James, Caroline Crabb, Lyn Davies, Pamela Wheeler, Dale Rogers, Marina Thomas and Kay Body.

224. Llanfoist County Primary School. Back row, left to right: Kay Mills, Nigel Hollister, John Bannon, Mark Williams, Lyn Boyt, Clive Hitchman, Tony Davies, Gareth Walker and Dawn Edwards. Middle row: Julie James, Julie Griffiths, Gail Shaw, Denise Hillerbrand, Mrs Ware, Helen Prosser, Julie Bannon, Janet Dickenson and Diane Hollaway. Front row: Kevin Badham, David Isaac, Phillip Chadwick and Lewis Richards.

225. The latest visitors to Crickhowell 1910. Outside T H Ward the corn merchants, the dancing bears perform just down the road from the Bear Hotel.

226. A little further down the road from where the dancing bears are standing, a large parade passes Townsend's Boot and Shoe store, with schoolchildren, scouts and soldiers all taking part. The Cambrian Arms has just recently been altered to widen the road.

227.   Crickhowell's new Post Office in 1909 pictured shortly after completion. The exterior of the building is much the same today except that the road surface has been greatly improved and widened.

228.   The tall figure of Lord Glanusk standing in front of the platform built around the Lucas monument, where the Prince of Wales, later to become King Edward VIII is addressing the crowd in 1925.

Acknowledgements

I wish to offer my sincerest thanks to my wife Bev for her help and encouragement during the production of this book; my children Nikki and Ben for putting up with my postcard obsession; Councillor Alan Breeze and Mr Peter Williams for the foreword.

I should also like to thank Mr Gwyn Jones and Miss Gladys Hughes, my history teachers at the Grammar School. Although not one of their best pupils, it was they who first sparked my interest in local history and I am forever grateful to them.

Thanks must also go to the following: Mr Bryan Roden another postcard enthusiast, for his most enjoyable company to the many postcard fairs held around the country; Mr Malcolm Thomas for his incitement and help in the publication of this book; Mr C Keohane and the late Mr Albert Lyons for all their encouragement.

For assisting with names and photographs I should like to thank my brother John and sister Julie; My mother and father-in-law, Reg and Eileen Jones; Mrs Carol Paten, Mr Andrew Hands, Roy Stockham, Mary Cummings and Adoree Flower.

My sincere apologies are extended to anyone who I may have inadvertently omitted.

The author would very much welcome the loan of any further photographs or postcards etc. from readers who might wish to see them included in a second volume of this book. He may be contacted at the address of the publishers.

Further books in this series are available from Bookshops or through The Publishers.

Blaenavon Through The Years in Photographs	**- Volume 1**
by Malcolm Thomas and John Lewis	ISBN 0 9512181 0 7
Blaenavon Through The Years in Photographs	**- Volume 2**
by Malcolm Thomas and John Lewis	ISBN 0 9512181 3 1
Blaenavon Through The Years in Photographs	**- Volume 3**
by Malcolm Thomas and John Lewis	ISBN 1 874538 10 7
Old Aberbeeg and Llanhilleth in Photographs	**- Volume 1**
by Bill Pritchard	ISBN 0 9512181 5 8
Old Aberbeeg and Llanhilleth in Photographs	**- Volume 2**
by Bill Pritchard	ISBN 1 874538 35 2
Blackwood Yesterday in Photographs	**- Book 1**
by Ewart Smith	ISBN 0 9512181 6 6
Blackwood Yesterday in Photographs	**- Book 2**
by Ewart Smith	ISBN 1 874538 65 4
A Look at Old Tredegar in Photographs	**- Volume 1**
by Philip Prosser	ISBN 0 9512181 4 X
A Portrait of Rhymney	**- Volume 1**
by Marion Evans	ISBN 1 874538 40 9
A Portrait of Rhymney	**- Volume 2**
by Marion Evans	ISBN 1 874538 70 0
Brynmawr, Beaufort and Blaina in Photographs	**- Volume 1**
by Malcolm Thomas	ISBN 1 874538 15 8
Caldicot and the Villages of the Moor	**- Volume 1**
by Malcolm D Jones	ISBN 1 874538 50 6
Talgarth - Jewel of the Black Mountains	**- Volume 1**
by Roger G. Williams	ISBN 1 874538 60 3
Trinant in Photographs	**- Volume 1**
by Clive Daniels	ISBN 1 874538 80 8

Also available are novels of local interest which include:
The Black Domain - *by Ralph Thomas*   ISBN 0 9512181 7 4
A portrayal of life and romance in 19th century industrial Blackwood with a balanced blend of fact and fiction.
The Land of Brychan - *by Nansi Selwood*   ISBN 1 874538 30 1
Set in 17th century Brecknock and Glamorgan, this is a novel full of richness of the life of the gentry class based on a fusion of fact and folk memory.
Folklore of Blaenau Gwent   ISBN 1 874538 85 9
A fascinating and definitive collection of centuries old legends and folklore from northern Monmouthshire.